# the Emotional Elf

Faye Farmer

**SECOND EDITION**

BooksElf Publishing 2019

Copyright © Faye Farmer 2019

**FIRST EDITION**

Melrose Books 2018

Copyright © Faye Farmer 2018

The Author asserts her moral right to
be identified as the author of this work


Cover designed by Faye Farmer & Nik Farmer
Emo drawn by Niki Farmer


**ISBN   978-1-9160703-0-1 Paperback**

**978-1-9160703-1-8 epub**

**978-1-9160703-2-5 mobi**

This book is a social skills story about family, love and communication.

I dedicate this book to my husband, Nik, and children, Joshua, Nikoletta, Jacob, Amy and all my extended family.

What a challenging but truly amazing Christmas.

I wrote this book to help deal with the Emotions and challenges that we have faced over the last couple of years.

I love you all greatly and I am proud of each and every one of you, and love you just as you are.

We have overcome so many challenges along our journey; many assessments, doctors and hospital appointments, diagnoses. We have been asked so many questions on very personal things, asked if our kids have been abused multiple times because of the behaviour they showed, and while I know it is important these questions get asked so no child that is abused falls through the net, it doesn't make it a pleasant experience. It is also something other parents of children with hidden disabilities experience; I have spoken to many who have also told me they have experienced this. We have been treated wrongly by many, excluded, and had our worries dismissed.

It has to stop. Parents don't want their children treated differently because of their struggles. Children just want to be heard and have their struggles seen and acted on from all the different professionals so they are given the same opportunities as everyone else, treated with respect and acceptance, and given guidance until they learn to self-regulate their Emotions.

So, along the journey toward all these diagnoses, parents lose a sense of who they are and they become disillusioned by the system. Lost and invisible to their struggles, not sure if they are doing to right thing to help, because they don't have the situation fully explained, they become tired and angry and shut down. It transfers to every part of their life; there is nothing to stop the roller coaster they have been thrown onto.

No one seems to know the best way, so they try everything they are told by the experts until their ability to just be a parent is stripped from them.

This is how my book began, learning to be Mum again, learning to forget every bit of advice, and learning to be the fun-loving mum and wife again. That is the hardest thing, the wife bit, because all of your focus is on trying to help your children, you forget you're part of a team.

You just fight to get through one day at a time, you push the one you love the most away because you are weak and don't want to let them down. You hide inside yourself because you feel you failed as a mum, you don't deserve nice things to happen to you, you punish yourself for their suffering and your inability to take it away.

I was broken but not destroyed, I was weak but now I am strong.

It is now my turn to be strong for all around me, till they are strong themselves again. Learning to trust again in my mother's instinct, which has been there the whole time, it was just disregarded as an over-anxious mother, and maybe I was, but when the tests confirm the things you already know in your heart to be true there is no denying the anger at having been dismissed so many times.

My book is a diary of mischievous elves.

This is a mother's quest, to be just Mum again.

From the 1st December 2016 till the 1st January 2017.

# Emo the Emotional Elf

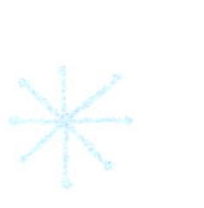

# Emo the Emotional Elf

# Day 1

Here is a little story to get Christmas on the way.

So, while the Farmer house was asleep, Emo the Emotional Elf came to visit. I could hear bells jingling outside our house, so opened the door to find Emo the Elf sitting among the candy canes.

He then thought it would be funny to climb through the letter box as he was in a really elfish mood.

He told me he was bursting for the toilet, so I showed him where it was. Emo then went to visit Niki and took some pictures while she was sound asleep.

He went to check on Jake. He was sound asleep as well, so he checked his computer to see what was happening in Minecraft world.

Emo, so as not to leave daddy out, took selfies with him while he was sleeping and took a shine to his iPhone.

Emo was so mischievous and wondered what he could get up to next, so he flirted with mummy, had a drink and nibbles, before swinging on a garland above the fireplace and eating the Christmas chocolates.

**Emo the Emotional Elf**

Emo placed Niki and Jake's advent calendars in the front room next to the Santa's workshop pillow, as it made him feel at home.

He is, after all, staying till New Year so he has many night-time adventures to get up to while the house is asleep.

Till tomorrow, sleep well, Farmer household.

**Your new friend. I love you all.**

*emo the emotional elf xx*

# Day 2

## Elfish behaviour

Emo has been up to no good tonight, he has been on an adventure looking for love and family and knowledge. While Jake and Niki have an adventure staying at Nan and Grandad's house for the night, Emo decided to have fun in their rooms while they were gone.

First though, he felt the happy feeling of a warm heart.

He was on a quest for knowledge so he discovered some books in Jake's room and learnt all about music, as it's something all the Farmer family love.

He also learnt about fast cars and daydreamed about being the next *Top Gear* presenter, or maybe even the next Stig.

He knows big bro Josh will be here for Christmas so wanted to learn more about astronomy as he knows Josh had a thing about aliens when he was Jake's age, he-he.

He was so excited to share his love with one of Niki's friends that he took her to the Christmas ball in his digger truck limo, but did get her back home by midnight as she might have turned back into a skeleton.

Emo decided to dress up in a rainbow tutu and ride on a pink flamingo.

Emo slid down the banister and made sweet music by swinging from the chandelier before having a snuggle with Dad.

He ran back upstairs to take a selfie with two special people, Pickles and Nanu, before reading the Bible as he knew when he had his late night chat with Yia-Yia on the phone she would want to talk about this as it is important to her.

Emo then did something very naughty and ate Daddy's Lion Bar, bad Emo; he passed out on the kitchen floor from sugar overload.

**Goodnight, Farmer family,
with love**

*emo the emotional elf xx*

Day 3

Emo the Elf has been busy tonight exploring
the Farmer household.

Emo had to be rescued by Mum as he was looking for
a missing stocking in the washing machine and the door
closed, he was banging on the door saying, 'Let me out,
let me out.'

Emo got into the Christmas window mood and changed
the word to Zelo. (Each year the Farmer family have letters
on the window and take turns to change
the words.)

He then spent a couple of
hours watching late night
shopping channels to
get present ideas to
tell Santa.

## Emo the Emotional Elf

Emo checked the naughty and nice list
to see if Josh has been good.

Emo is a really cheeky elf and wanted to ask
Angel out on a date.

Emo wondered if Dad wanted help with putting
up the curtain pole.

Emo was wondering what jobs around the house Mum might
need to do and decided she should do the ironing; Mum
screamed and hid in the cupboard.

He will also remind Mum not to
be a complete numpty and
lock keys in the house
again, that's why Dad
put up a key rack; to
make sure there is
not a mad stressful
rush to find them,
he-he, as Mum has
the memory of a
sieve.

Emo relaxed against the Emoji pillows while blaring out Black Veil Bride's music as Niki was away for the night.

Emo used Niki's room to play a bit of hide and seek with her dolls.

Emo was amazed at all the Lego Jake had created and displayed in his room.

Emo lay on Jake's bed because he wanted to catch up on reading the Harry Potter book, as reading is so important.

Emo then researched space and maps of Europe so that when he goes back to the North Pole he can tell all the other elves what he learnt so they can support Santa more. Santa works so hard all year to make sure children get their presents.

Till tomorrow, dear Farmer family.

**I love you all.**

*emo the emotional elf  xxx*

# Day 4

Emo the Emotional Elf got called back to the North Pole by Santa; he had a call from Santa and had to go to the phone box at the end of the street to call him back.

It was a top secret mission and he didn't want the Farmer family to hear what Santa had said.

So he didn't get any pictures last night. Emo went on a mission with Mum and jumped into her beautiful handbag she got from Yia-Yia for her birthday. They were going to get some pics this morning while Jake and Niki were asleep.

**Emo the Emotional Elf**

First, Emo and Mum scraped the car, Emo loved it because he could feel the cold snow all around him and it reminded him of the snow at the North Pole.

Emo the Elf got in the car and put on his seat belt, a very important job so he could be safe, after all, Mum is driving, he-he.

Mum and Emo drove over to the shops and took a selfie in front of the church Mum and Dad got married in.

Emo then escorted Mum to the cash point to get some money to send to Santa for presents. Emo helped Mum with the shopping, although he could have carried the basket instead of making it heavier by sitting in it, lazy Emo.

Emo went to give Grandad his tools back as the Farmer family really appreciated the loan of them.

Emo tried to sneak into Grandad's house by climbing up the trellis, but Grandad's security cameras zoomed in and he didn't want his face caught on the video, so he decided to knock on the door instead.

The problem with turning up early is that you surprise your Aunty Hayley when she is half asleep, just to take a selfie, I don't think she was impressed.

Emo and Mum stayed for a quick coffee
and chat with Grandad before
getting back in the car and
going to the park, you see,
Emo the Greedy Emotional
Elf decided to stuff himself
with lots of chocolate
which made him
extremely hyperactive,
so Mum took Emo to
the park to burn some
energy. Before they left
the park, Emo got caught
short and needed a wee,
but he couldn't find a toilet so
had to use a hedge.

Emo really enjoyed the outing with
Mum and came home calm and contented.

Good night Farmer family.

**I love you all.**

*emo the emotional elf  xxx*

# Day 5

Emo the Emotional Elf had another fabulous evening taking selfies with Mum. Emo took selfies with Mum because he thought she was cute with her new hair. Emo thought it gave her a bit of sparkle.

Emo helped Mum to fold up the napkins and had his picture taken with the wall plaque which says 'you are brave'.

Emo the Emotional Elf thinks the writing on the plaque represents the Farmer family and should be the family motto.

Emo then sat and listened to Mum telling him the nativity story and took pics with Santa and the snowman before trying to eat Jake's chocolate from his advent calendar. Mum caught him and told him off.

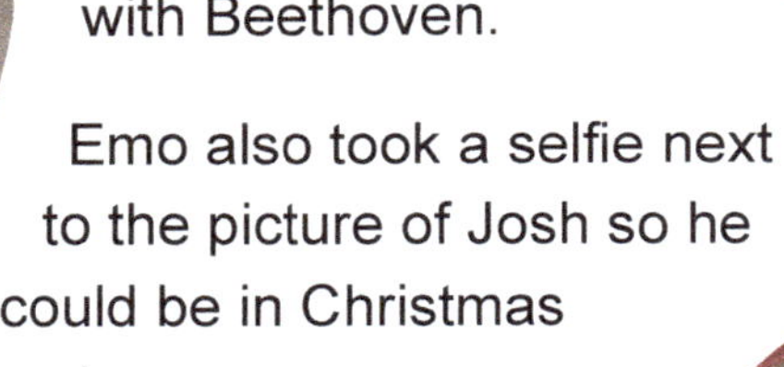

He rode a reindeer to have a selfie with Beethoven.

Emo also took a selfie next to the picture of Josh so he could be in Christmas story too.

In the morning, Emo decided to get Niki dressed as an elf and take selfies with her and then drop her off for her school bus.

Emo was so pleased by Jake and Niki's behaviour this morning while they were at school he baked them some elf cookies.

Until tomorrow, Farmer family.

**I love you all.**

*emo the emotional elf xxx*

# Day 6

**Emo the Emotional Elf**

Emo the Emotional Elf started the night by
keeping Mum company while Dad worked.
Mum keeps watch till Dad comes home.

Emo decided Mum needed more upper
body strength in order to lift the big
gammon out of the freezer in time for
Christmas day, so he helped her do
some press-ups, after he messed about
in the garden and
tried climbing
on the porch
to peek in
Jake's window to
see if he was asleep.

Emo the Emotional Elf had a disagreement with Angel on top of the tree, to see who looked better; I guess Angel has a strong character like Niki and pushed him off, LOL.

Emo had to check his naughty-or-nice list; I guess Niki, Josh, Tom and Jake made the good list. Mum and Dad were not so lucky and didn't.

Emo thought they should try harder and work together to get back in Santa's good books.

**Emo the Emotional Elf**

Emo the Emotional Elf is such a softie for charities he
decided to promote Children in Need by wearing Jake's
Pudsey bear ears.

Emo the Emotional Elf decided he
wanted to know what it felt like
to have big feet like Josh so
put on Mum's elf shoes.

As always, Emo was
hungry, so had a
pizza and coke
night. He thinks
Niki's friend,
Grace, would
have liked to
join that party
because it was
cool and Grace
loves pizza.

Mum thought Emo ate too much. She went to check to see if Dad was home, and when she came back to the kitchen she caught Emo red-handed with his hands in the bag of sweets Niki had made at school. Mum said, "You're a bad boy Emo," But how could mum be cross for long with those sweet eyes looking at her.

Mum thinks Dad had better watch out for Emo the Elf as he has ideas above his station and has a tiny crush on Mum. He even plumbed the address for the North Pole into her satnav. Good job Dad understands that Mum is loyal and in love with him.

Until tomorrow, Farmer family.

**I love you all.**

emo the emotional elf xxx

# Day 7

Emo the Emotional Elf had a relaxing day at home while Mum took Jake to school and Dad to work, and drove Niki to her school as she'd missed the school bus.

Dad had told Mum to get some sleep the night before as she would probably oversleep. He was right, but Mum liked staying up waiting for Dad to come home from work, she was excited to see him just like all the nights she waited up to see him when he was a DJ at a nightclub.

Emo started the evening by setting table for dinner, it was so nice that Mum, Dad, Niki and Jake were all eating together and laughing, this made Mum's eyes sparkle and filled her with happiness.

While Mum watched *Holby City* with Jake, Niki was talking to Tom: Emo went outside to play.

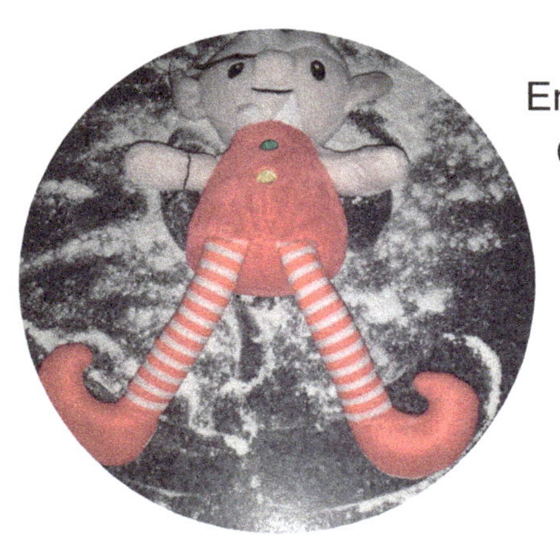

Emo decided to create his own Christmas scene and make snow angels; he got so cold he had to call Mum to warm him up.

So Mum tried with an emergency survival blanket she got from Joshua's Duke of Edinburgh kit, when that didn't work, Emo thought he would go for a spin in the microwave (don't try this at home kids, it's dangerous).

Still his feet were cold so he put the heating on and used his puppy dog eyes to persuade Mum to make him an Ovaltine drink.

Emo decided to get a red trumpet and play 'When the Saints Go Marching In'. Mum was not happy: Dad woke up.

Emo took Bernard the dog for a ride before sharing a Christmas cracker with him.

Emo thought he would impress Niki by playing a word game.

Emo the Elf's first word was 'max' as he wants to live life to the max; his second word was 'lemon' because he acts like a lemon sometimes.

Emo the Emotional Elf found that love is all one really needs.

Emo wanted to hide in Dad's jacket as it was so warm and cosy he felt safe.

Emo said, "Good night," to the Farmer Family.

Emo the Emotional Elf signing out till tomorrow.

**I love you all.**

xxx

# Day 8

Emo the Emotional Elf snuck out of the house and into Dad's shed and took Jake's bike for a spin. Mum was cross because he didn't put on his helmet, so she gave him a ten minute time out in the corner. Mum said, "You're a bad boy, Emo." Emo was sad so he went to share his feelings of sadness with the angels, who explained to him the importance of wearing a helmet and that Mum loves him and doesn't want him to get hurt.

He thought he would check Evelyn and Niki were asleep before he could have a peek on Niki's computer; Emo wants to make sure she is being responsible.

Emo was wondering how on earth the neighbours didn't hear the sleep hypnosis video Mum played to try and help her family sleep as she wired Dad's large speaker into her phone.

Emo photo-bombed the Christmas pictures of Niki and Jake with Santa, before admiring Niki's drawings that have pride of place on Mum's fridge.

He then got hungry so had a snatch and grab of Jacob's Pringles. "He-he, yum-yum," said Emo.

The only problem with Emo staying
at the Farmer household
is that he will need to
diet on crackers after
Christmas, as he
won't be such a
small elf: he will be
bigger than Santa.
Emo understands
that Josh will
be home for
Christmas so
he got to the
ice cream first
because Josh loves
his ice cream and
can eat a whole tub in
one sitting.

Emo decided to try out for a
rock band by playing the drums.

Billy Bones, the skeleton that Jake had been making
to learn about his body, was so hungry he decided to try
to eat Emo.

Emo likes to see that Jacob is saving money, he is learning the value of it, and how important having some money saved for a rainy day is.

Emo was feeling mighty, so he decided to try and take on none other than Superman. He was still in play-fighting mood and remembered Santa told him about the time Josh jumped off the table bushwhacker style, and tried to wrap his legs round Dad's neck to get him over. So Emo tried to do it with Robosapiens.

About half an hour later, Mum and Dad heard the biggest, highest pitched screaming. They ran upstairs to find Emo hanging off Jake's light as he saw a big spider on the pillow. I guess Mum is the only one in the house strong enough to handle spiders.

I must admit, the spider was bigger than the 'daddy-no-like' ones. They're called that because Daddy no like it when Mum throws them at him, ha-ha.

Emo then found the most comfortable duck bed, it was a Hug-Duck slipper, to relax in while he studied triple science because he wanted to be a marine biologist like Jake does.

Emo the Emotional Elf wants to let the Farmer household in on a big secret. The reason for the stripy tights is elves' hatred of having hairy legs in Lapland and they don't stock wax strips, so that is the reason all elves wear stockings.

Good night to my dearest friends, the Farmer family, until tomorrow.

**I love you all.**

*emo the emotional elf xxx*

# Day 9

Emo the Elf was so excited, just as much as Jake and Niki, when Santa showed up at the door. The loud screams and the wind created as Emo, Niki and Jake went running out of the house, nearly sending Mum flying in their wake, to Santa on his slay playing Christmas songs and handing out sweets to all the children and asking them whether they have been good or bad.

He also reminded Emo not to eat too much sugar, or he will not be able to stop jumping up and down. That he will stop Niki and Jake from sleeping because Santa said, "Niki and Jake already have sleep issues and it is not healthy to not sleep."

Emo decided he would do his elf story with Mum because he got back late.

Mum had a very busy day yesterday and is tired this morning.

But she must carry on; so much to do. Jake is at school and got up early as he has an interview to be head teacher for the day. Emo and Mum, Dad and Niki are wishing him the best of luck and telling him to be strong and confident.

Dad is on holiday from work and is really helping Mum by just being there and looking after Niki who is off school with a bad headache. He also picked Jake up from school yesterday, so Mum could watch Niki's school play.

Niki's part in the school play was so funny and brought the house down. She should be as proud of herself as Mum and Dad are of her.

Emo and Mum are on a mission to get as much done as possible.

As Mum has work tonight, Emo made sure she had breakfast and ate her fruit to keep her energy up.

Mum and Emo went to Grandad's to look after Aunty Hayley who is ill with flu while Grandad did his food shopping.

Emo and Mum decided to rummage through Niki and Jake's rooms at Grandad's house and play with their toys. First, in Niki's room, Emo got frustrated with the Rubik's Cube so decided to hang out with the Adventure Time Crew.

Emo the Elf loves Elsa and Anna from the film 'Frozen' and tried to marry Anna off to a superhero to mend Anna's Frozen Heart, just like in the film, only true love can unfreeze the heart.

Emo loved looking at Niki's photos and thinks she is so beautiful she could be a model.

Emo likes all sides of Niki's personality, so took a selfie with her skull. Which is an ornament which shows some of Niki's Gothic side.

Emo wanted to build a snowman.

Emo decided to crack the code on Grandad's door, he-he.

Emo the Elf decided to go into Jake's room next.

He found Dave the monkey crying because he was sad and lonely without Jake and Josh, so he picked him up and put him on his knee and sung 'You Raise Me Up', as this is a song Jake loves Mum to sing to him when he is feeling sad.

The next thing Emo did was set up
the backgammon board, and
he wants to challenge Aunty
Ellie to a game as he
understands she is very
good at this game, but
can she beat him?

Emo likes challenges
and, so as not to
leave anyone out,
wants to challenge
Mia, Izzy and Molly to
a 'Datty Wine' dance
when he sees them.

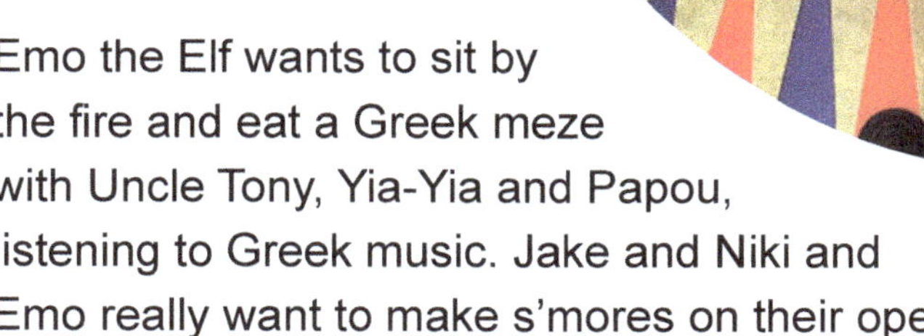

Emo the Elf wants to sit by
the fire and eat a Greek meze
with Uncle Tony, Yia-Yia and Papou,
listening to Greek music. Jake and Niki and
Emo really want to make s'mores on their open fire.

So this is the end of the story tonight, Farmer family,
until tomorrow.

**I love you all.**

*emo the emotional elf  xxx*

# Day 10-11

Emo and the Farmers were invaded by the Hords.

Emo and the Farmers were so excited that they had their cousins Ellie, Tom and Holly coming to stay for the night.

It was going to be a night of elfish fun.

When the pyjama-clad Hords came,
Jake, Niki, Mum and Dad were
happy.

Mad selfies with the elfies were
taken before camping out in
Mum and Dad's
room to sing
Christmas
songs and
watch *Polar
Express* with a bag full of
popcorn. After the movie was
finished, Mum and Emo read
the story of how the gnomes

saved the day
and helped the elves,
before everyone snuggled
down together and slept;
peaceful day.

# Day 12

Emo the Emotional Elf
and his brother, Derrick
the Elf, started the night
taking selfies with Mum.

Emo the Elf wanted to
travel the solar system on
his homemade Coca-Cola
rocket; he had such fun.

Next, Emo and Derrick played
Pokéball, they wanted to see which of them
could catch them all.

Emo and Derrick played the window challenge,
they got lemons and snow and almost got into
an argument when they spelt the word 'snore', over

which one of them snores the loudest.

Emo thought it would be funny to lay his brother down and take a selfie himself while making an impression of Derrick's face with a Pin Art board.

After Derrick managed to get out, he told Emo he'd found a mouse in the garden and had brought it in to show him.

To say Emo screamed would be an understatement, it shook the house so hard the Farmer family thought it was an earthquake.

Emo thought he would take a chocolate bath as he'd heard it was good for his skin on a Facebook post. He believes everything he reads, and he was so sticky Mum had to help him clean himself up, she said to Emo, "You can't believe everything you read on Facebook."

Next, Emo decided to try a puzzle, but got so frustrated he had an anxiety attack and squeezed himself into a jug to calm down.

Emo and Derrick wish the Farmer family a good night.

**We love you all.**

# Day 13

**Emo the Emotional Elf**

Emo the Emotional Elf and Derrick the Elf wanted to spend the day in Brighton, Christmas shopping with Mum and Niki.

First, they jumped in Mum's bag for the short walk to the car.

Niki made sure that Emo and Derrick were buckled up in their seat belts, but the cheeky elves kept getting out and admiring the view from the window.

They loved looking at the countryside as they drove up and down the small hills and winding roads. It did make them a little sick to the stomach, though, but the travel sickness pills worked and kept the sickness from splurging all over the car and Mum. Mum knows from the experience of travel sickness herself, when she first met her brother-in-law, Tony; she was sick as a dog and just missed him.

## Emo the Emotional Elf

Emo and Derrick took a selfie on a signpost first of all, so they can show the elves where Niki's school was. Niki's school has lots of beautiful, special children. Mum and Emo see their potential, and their smiles make them so great to be around and Niki has made many friends there and enjoys helping out.

When Mum, Niki, Emo and Derrick first got to Brighton, they were hungry so they all stopped and had a McDonald's.

Derrick the Elf got a bit addicted to the ketchup and we had to drag him away.

We looked around the shops and saw a Lego shop. Derrick the Elf and Emo got creative and created Santa out of the Lego.

We then took a look at the Christmas decorations and saw a beautiful wishing tree. The tree had tags hanging on it for children to write their names and what they would like for Christmas. Mum, Niki, Emo and Derrick thought it was a great idea, but it is the giving nature of others choosing one and gifting it, for those children to receive a present.

As we think everyone deserves a present at Christmas.

We all then posed for selfies before we saw an awesome present for Josh, we also saw a dome of lights.

Emo and Derrick were with Niki when one of her dreams came true and she got to build a bear at the Build-a-Bear workshop and choose outfits for it. Niki cried tears of joy, so Emo and Derrick wanted to share the moment with a picture. We then walked back along the seafront to the minibus and admired the view on the way back.

Emo and Derrick also found time to make an elf Christmas cake for the Farmer family.

**Love you all, till tomorrow.**

# Day 14

Emo the Emotional Elf and Derrick have been up to mischief again.

Derrick the Elf was riding the Rudolf that Jake had made out of wood at school, to get in practice for the Christmas Eve present marathon.

First, Emo and Derrick played hide and seek. Emo hid in the food cupboard, no surprises there, and Derrick hid in a napkin. Mum was peeking and found them easily; she knows everything; she seems to have eyes in the back of her head.

Emo and Derrick were both dropping the hint about food again, but Mum would not give them any more as they didn't eat all their dinner.

They're naughty elves as they have stolen the cake, you know, the one that says stollen on the pack.

Emo and Derrick were playing the odd one out game, it wasn't really a game, it was a way for Mum to get the socks in pairs, she challenged them to see who would be able to do it quicker, the one with the odd sock left at the end would lose. It was Derrick, he had a big meltdown because sometimes he and Emo have difficulties playing games and following rules and really they are just bad at losing.

Emo and Derrick think mum deserves to be centre stage in the elves' Christmas production *The Nutcracker*.

Just when you least expected it, Derrick came in like a wrecking ball, he thought he was Miley, he-he. He was swinging from the Christmas bauble.

Derrick wanted to help Dad out; as you know all dads at Christmas get upset when old-style lights get tangled, or bulbs don't work. It can be frustrating, so he has been watching what Dad does to fix lights and replaces the bulbs for him under Mum's watchful eye. She knows Jake knows his health and safety rules, because Dad taught him. Jake would stand there and tell them if they weren't being safe.

Emo watched while Derrick tried to fit into a berry tutu, i.e. a napkin ring, but suffered a lot of embarrassment, as a lot of ladies and gentleman know; we grow a little bigger at Christmas. Derrick was upset because it got stuck on his legs, and Emo was rolling on the floor laughing.

Next, guess who played pie face? Emo got the pie in the face but so did Derrick, Mum could not resist, as it's not kind to laugh at others bad luck so she pushed his face in it just like she did to Niki, when she was at the Pizza Hut and was messing about her. Niki and Grace laughed so much at Mum's playfulness.

But kids, don't feel sorry for the elves, as Mum said that they were very hyperactive all day.

Last of all Derrick and Emo fed Rudolf hot chilli sauce, because Santa's sleigh needed a bit of extra wind to help keep them on the right course and Brussels leave a nasty smell in the air just like what happens in the car on the after-school run and everyone has to be driven home with heads out of windows, just think, poor Santa has had thousands of years of smelling Brussels.

Emo and Derrick say, "Good night dear Farmer family."

**Emo the Emotional Elf and Derrick the Elf, until tomorrow, we love you all to the moon and back.**

# Day 15

Emo the Elf, Derrick the Elf and Dad decided to arrange the window display. Because Emo was hungry, Emo and Derrick thought they might eat Jake's cookies.

Next, Emo and Derrick the Elves checked out the roof on Jake's house in the garden, just in case Santa landed there instead.

Emo and Derrick thought they might play tug of war with the skipping rope when Mum, being clumsy, fell over it.

Then, bad Emo decided to play with a plastic bow and arrow and fired the arrow at his brother Derrick. It wasn't meant to happen that way, but the arrow went through Derrick's shirt and the sticky plunger on the end stuck to the fridge, leaving Derrick hanging by the arrow to the fridge door.

Emo and Derrick had a war over words about who left the Brussels smell in kitchen. Mum was not pleased and put them behind bars, in other words, tied them to the garden gate; that's the elves, not Niki and Jake.

**Emo the Emotional Elf**

They broke free and tried to climb up to Jacobs's window but couldn't reach so they decided to knock on the front window to get Dad's attention. Dad let them in and got into the elves' mood with them and had selfies with the Elfie's.

Last of all, Emo and Derrick want to let Holly know they will give her back her Paw Patrol dogs when they next see her.

That's it for today.

Good night Emo and Derrick the Elves.

**Until tomorrow, Farmer family, we love you all.**

# Day 16

# Emo the Emotional Elf

Emo the Emotional Elf and Derrick the Elf have been having fun today, it's Christmas jumper day, Jake and Mum dressed as elves for the day.

Niki got to wear a Christmas Grinch jumper.

Mum wore her elf costume everywhere and got so many smiles and people wanting to help her. I think she was sharing the Christmas spirit with everyone.

Mum wants to thank Dad for cooking her a beautiful dinner; her tummy feels so full.

Emo and Derrick went to help Jacob and Mum look after Tom, Holly and Ellie at Grandad's house.

They had lots of fun hiding in Grandad's Christmas tree and swinging from his ceiling fan.

Emo and Derrick wanted to be a table decoration so they hid among the tinsel and candle display.

Emo and Derrick love having sleepovers at Grandad's and used napkins as sleeping bags.

Next, Emo and Derrick took a picture with the Hord family coat of arms because the Hords are really important to the Farmer family.

Emo and Derrick wanted to have a boxing match before wrestling with Buzz Lightyear.

Emo and Derrick took a picture next to Grandad's fishing picture as Grandad's too cool to pose with them; they took selfies with the Buddha of Wealth to bring luck in the lottery tonight.

They blared out the music in Grandad's front room and found Grandad's secret bottle of wine.

Emo, Derrick and the children sung Christmas songs to give Mum the energy to pump up Tommy's bed. My goodness she had muscles like a rock when she finished.

Emo and Derrick did a midnight raid on Grandad's food cupboard and stole Jacobs crackers. Jake was not impressed.

Emo and Derrick found one of Joshua's ties; one more to add to your collection, Josh.

Emo and Derrick want to challenge Josh, Bob and Matt to *Call of Duty* game, but realise they are all working really hard. Before Emo and Derrick finish today's story, they want to let Niki, Jake and Josh know that your family loves you.

Emo and Derrick want to let all the family know that we welcome a new addition, little Sofia, to our family. The joy of a new baby, especially at Christmas, brings hope and new meaning of family. She is beautiful just like her mum, Anna. Emo can't wait to meet them both and little Chloe. Mum would like to say that our families might not get together 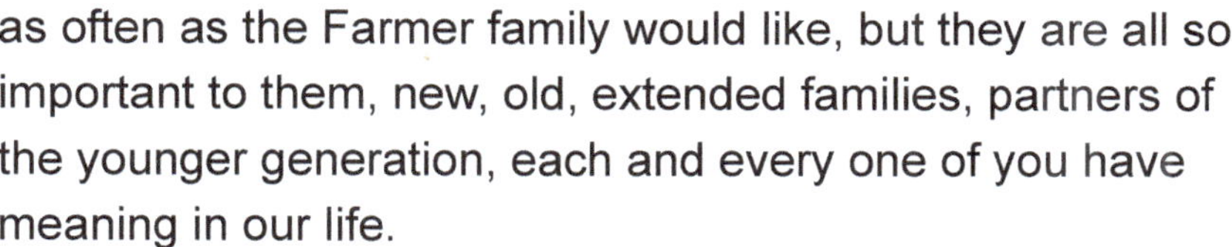 as often as the Farmer family would like, but they are all so important to them, new, old, extended families, partners of the younger generation, each and every one of you have meaning in our life.

So Emo and Derrick would like to wish the Farmer family and all the extended family a beautiful night.

**Love you all.**

xxx

# Day 17

Emo and Derrick, the very mischievous elves, played hide and seek with Jacob last night; it took Mum half an hour to find them.

Derrick was hiding in Grandad's tree and Emo had jumped into bed with Tom.

Next, Emo and Derrick got a little offended as dad had done the Christmas window word of the day and thought he was calling them moles, he-he.

Emo and Derrick thought they would pay Dad back by eating his lEmon puffs, so Mum told them off and made them eat their six fruit and veg, only problem was, she didn't mean all in one go and it gave them an upset tummy. So they were in the toilet for ages.

Derrick was teasing Emo again by eating the pistachio nuts.

Emo and Derrick looked in to their crystal ball to see what Santa was up to. When I say crystal ball, what I mean is snow globe, when elves shake it they see the real Lapland.

Next, Derrick knew Emo needed a good hair cut before Christmas but knew Emo wanted to grow his hair long so he taped his older brother to the table and did it anyway.

Mum says, "Kids, don't try this at home," it should be done by an adult. Emo and Derrick then had to record their heights as Santa doesn't want tall elves as they won't fit in the workshop.

Emo and Derrick are like most human kids and end up playing more with the box than the present that came in it.

Emo wanted to stargaze with Derrick, but
what Derrick didn't know was he had
been waiting all day long to get him
back for the pranks he played
on him, so he'd put black
soot on the eye piece
of the telescope.

Emo put on his glasses
before reading Derrick
some of Dad's *Top Gear*
book. Mum had to remind him to clean his
glasses.

Derrick, not being able to let his brother play the
last trick of the night decided to pretend he brought Emo an
iPhone, but really it was an empty box, and when
Emo opened it he squirted him with cream.
Mum was on the floor laughing.

Good night, dear Farmer family,
until tomorrow.

**We love you**

*emo and derrick*

# Day 18

This is tomorrow, but as Mum has had a few Malibus, we thought we'd better write it before she zonked out.

First, Emo and Derrick painted a message on the tree Aunty Hayley made for them out of wood at the day centre, while Mum took Aunty Hayley to do her Christmas shopping. Mum was so impressed with how the house looked when she came home and how clean Niki's room was, she fainted on the floor. She told Emo and Derrick it made her feel happy that Dad had cleaned the kitchen, and Jake and Niki their rooms. Her family was making good progress.

Next, they watched while Mum set the table and made dinner.

Emo and Derrick were greedily watching and hoping there would be leftovers for them when everyone went to sleep.

Emo and Derrick let their male testosterone show, and Mum gave them a hug because she likes that.

Next, they thought Niki had school tomorrow so hid in her school bag; she got a surprise when she opened it to put her lunch in.

Emo and Derrick love the new messages Mum put on the fridge.

Emo and Derrick used the Christmas garland as a swing.

Emo and Derrick found a pot of gold which they think the fairies left for them to give to the children (chocolate coins).

Emo and Derrick wanted to make sure that Santa Tracker was working so checked on the computer, while on there they looked at homeless shelters that the kids could give some things to so they learn that Christmas is as much about giving and not just about receiving. Because giving to those less fortunate and making someone feel they are cared for, even if they don't feel it, is a really good thing, and Emo and Derrick told Santa about the lesson the kids really understood so Santa put them higher on the good list.

Next, they thought they would give Angel a flower and Derrick decided to dance with her, while Emo sung 'Lady in Red', her favourite song, because the angel wore a beautiful red dress.

Lastly, they remembered to check the fridge for leftovers, Emo grabbed the spaghetti bolognaise he loved so much.

While Derrick grabbed the carrots, he, at least, listened to mum when she said, "Vegetables are good for you."

Good night Farmer family, until tomorrow.

**Love you all.**

# Day 19

Emo and Derrick the Elves started the night off with a jolly song with Frosty the Snowman then had a chat with Santa.

Emo and Derrick decided to have some fun, but heard a noise coming from Niki's room so decided to switch off the internet shaking their heads saying, "Teenagers these days." Emo and Derrick next went into kitchen to check out the window word of the day: Dad had changed it to 'lanes'.

Emo and Derrick are excited about Christmas and try to sneak a peek at Tom's presents under the tree that Niki wrapped.

Emo and Derrick tried to play the childhood game Roll the Ball, but had to use a walnut. Unfortunately, Derrick rolled it too hard and caught Emo in his elf place, which made Derrick laugh and facepalm. When Derrick finished laughing, he decided to get into the Farmer family's dab stance.

Emo and Derrick roasted chestnuts on the open fire; they sat around the candle they were using as fire, telling ghost stories without realising that a ghost had appeared beside Emo. They were so scared they made for the stairs to run away, Mum was laughing behind them while she Rick-rolled them. ('Never Gonna Give You Up'.)

Emo and Derrick were deciding which shoes to wear tomorrow when they noticed the fluffy hood on Dad's coat and thought it might make a nice bed and so they snuggled down in there for the night.

Emo and Derrick went to bathroom and Derrick gave his big brother Emo a shave. (Again kids, Mum, says, "Don't do this at home.")

They then went into Jacobs's room and lit up the Minecraft torch so they could search for some fun.

Emo and Derrick had a race, Pokémon verses My Little Pony: Pokémon won of course.

Next, they built a cup tower. Who would have thought the clumsy elves would have been able to do it? But they did: a tall tower, ten wide at the bottom to the one at the top.

Emo, of course, had to help his little brother get himself unstuck from the middle of the Sellotape roll, just as Mum had to help Niki out of the Sellotape roll earlier that evening; she put both her hands through it and got them stuck. Mum, Dad, Emo and Derrick tried to control their laughter, but failed. Niki, instead of getting stressed, joined in.

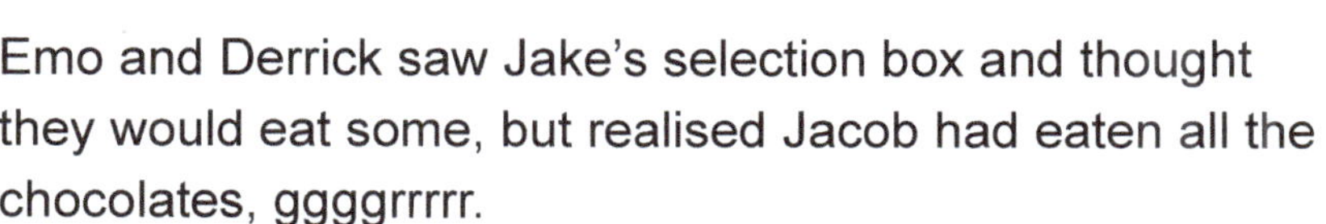

Emo and Derrick saw Jake's selection box and thought they would eat some, but realised Jacob had eaten all the chocolates, ggggrrrrr.

Lastly, Emo and Derrick thought they would try on the Christmas glasses and challenge Dad to recording a fun music video with them. Mum loved it so much; Dad always makes her laugh.

**Good night Farmer family,
love you all.**

emo and derrick the elves xxx

# Day 20

Emo and Derrick were buzzing; they could see the joy on Mum's face because Joshua, her oldest son, would be home today. Emo and Derrick heard he was a big lad, so thought they would be very careful what tricks they played on him while he is home.

Niki and Mum will be outnumbered by male testosterone on Christmas Eve as there will be Dad, Josh, Tom and Jake, Emo and Derrick. A very male house meaning the boys outnumbered the girls.

Emo and Derrick came with
Mum to pick Josh up
from the train station.
When they got
there, they took
a big gulp and
looked at each
other. They
could not
believe the
size of the
oldest Farmer
son. He was
huge, over six
foot tall with feet
of an elf giant,
but Josh, being the
leader, soon made
them feel at ease and took
a selfie with them. I'm sure
they will become the best of buddies.

When Emo, Derrick, Mum and Josh got home, Niki, Jake
and Dad were happy to see Josh. it took ages to get them
to go to bed; the excitement of this big brother's return was
almost too much to bear as they'd missed him while he had
been away.

Derrick and Emo looked at the window challenge and it said 'no meals'. Mum never knew elves could eat that much, so they drank all the milk and Coke instead.

Derrick was talking to Gabby the angel and that made Emo put his head on his knees and cry because he is the older brother and thought he could talk to her first.

Emo and Derrick helped Josh do his press-ups; they climbed on his back.

Josh gave them tips on rock climbing so they could climb the cupboards in search of food. Oh boy, Mum forgot Josh had a mischievous side.

Emo acted like a complete numpty, like Niki, and got his head stuck in the Sellotape.

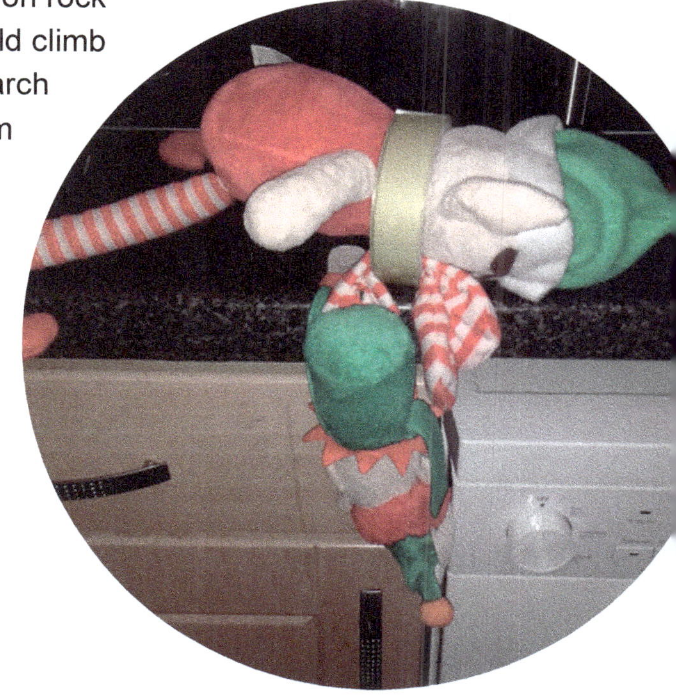

Emo thought he would get Derrick
back for talking to Gabby first,
so he pinched his nose with
a pair of pliers.

Dad went to the toilet and
Emo and Derrick thought
they would have a nose on
Dad's computer.

Emo and Derrick went
outside to see who could
hang upside down on
the Farmer family sign the
longest. Josh thought it would
be funny to lock them out, but they
were small enough
to climb through
the letter box.

Emo and Derrick were admiring the picture of Yia-Yia; Derrick really took a shine to it, you better watch out, Papou, as Derrick likes Yia-Yia a lot.

Next, they thought they would read some of Mum's romance books. We could all hear them giggling, like when boys first have the birds and bees talk, hahaha.

Emo and Derrick thought Mum might like help cleaning, so they went to the cleaning cupboard to see what they could do and got so frustrated by how Mum stacked it. They looked at each other and said, "No way." When they got bored, they radioed Santa on the walky-talky to see what their elf friends were doing.

Emo and Derrick want to wish the Farmer family the very best of nights.

**Love you all until tomorrow,**

*emo and derrick the elves*

# Day 21-22

Emo and Derrick was so busy helping Mum last night with some wrapping they just all fell asleep before doing their story, so here is one for both days.

Emo and Derrick helped Mum make dinner and set the table.

Next, Emo and Derrick want to say they tried the jar game; those who played it will know all about it. (Not mentioning any names, Nik and Tony.) He-he, naughty, naughty, Brussels in your stockings.

Emo and Derrick then had a wrestling match. Derrick may be smaller, but he has great flexibility due to his hypermobility.

Derrick and Emo wanted to try and be a Christmas cracker.

They also pretended to be decorations on the fireplace.

Emo and Derrick found Santa's bell ready to go on the Christmas Eve tray and would not stop ringing it till Mum took it off them.

They then went in search of food, and to their delight they found Mum had stocked the fridge. There was a massive turkey, woohoo.

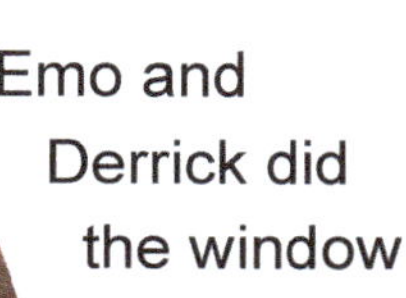

Emo and Derrick did the window challenge. Emo and Derrick used the ladder to try and reach Niki's window to make sure she was tidying her room – you know that it's Christmas week and Santa likes all kids to have clean rooms.

Emo wanted to lift some weights, but Derrick was not being any help as he was sitting on them.

Jake was playing catch the flying elf. Josh was using them like paper airplanes.

Lastly, Emo and Derrick wanted to give the Farmer family some tickets to the circus at the theatre on 7th of January – they hope they enjoy it.

Good night, Farmer family.

**Love you all.**

# Day 23

Emo and Derrick got called back to help Santa, as there was a mad rush to get Santa's sack filled, and he needed their help. They were there with a click of their fingers. When they returned, Emo and Derrick the Elves had had a busy day preparing and helping Mum and Dad get ready for Tom's arrival and be ready for Santa.

Tom arrived early this morning. Niki was so excited she ran and jumped into his arms. When they got back home, Niki made Tom a bacon sandwich while Mum popped to Grandad's to do a few last minute things on her list.

When Mum returned home, she changed into an elf outfit with Jake putting on his elf ears. Dad, Mum and Jake decided they didn't want Yia-Yia and Papou and Tony not to have presents to open in the morning, so it was decided Emo, Derrick, Jake and Mum would deliver their presents to them. So off on a journey went the elves, Mum and Jake to surprise the family and deliver presents in time for Christmas.

Yia-Yia and Papou were so surprised, that when Mum phoned when they got there and told them there were elves at their door, they were shocked. Emo and Derrick hid all over Yia-Yia's house.

Yia-Yia became acquainted with Emo the Elf and helped Jake feed them tea in her best, fine bone china she keeps in case of important visitors. Sometimes we think she would actually like the Queen to come.

Emo, Mum, Derrick and Jake put the presents under the tree.

Mum took a selfie with Yia-Yia and the elf, Jake took pictures with Yia-Yia's hats, you know the furry ones that often get mistaken for cats.

Before Jake, Mum, Emo and
Derrick left, they needed
a nap so they chilled
on uncle Tony's bed.
When they woke up
and left Yia-Yia's
house to go home,
Emo and Derrick
decided to cause
a commotion,
climbing up trees
outside in the
front garden on
the way to the car.
Yia-Yia said, "Get
down. What will my
neighbours think?" She
then made the sign of the
cross, something she does a lot
when she is worried, or not best pleased
about something.

**Good night sweet Farmer family. Love you all.**

*emo and derrick*

# Day 24

**Christmas Eve**

Emo and Derrick helped Jake write a card for Santa and prepare Santa's tray. It's so full of goodies and treats it's hard to see how Santa will ever fit back up the chimney.

Emo, Derrick and Jake put the key outside for Santa, just in case he couldn't fit through the chimney, before they hid in the stockings waiting for Santa.

Good night, children, be good and go to sleep as Santa will be here soon and he won't leave presents if you are awake.

OMG, Santa, Mum, Dad and Josh, Emo and Derrick have been so busy tonight. Dad and Mum and Josh have been in the kitchen sorting things for tomorrow. Dad is cooking the gammon and the lamb, Mum is in heaven: she just loves Dad's lamb, it melts in her mouth and makes her dribble, especially the juice it produces. I think if Dad is not quick, she might eat the lot. Dad smiles because he knows the way to his wife's heart is his food.

Happy Christmas everyone, woohoo, but I do hope kids sleep in tomorrow, we are so tired.

Doesn't anyone tell Santa to wipe his feet before he traipses his big, dirty shoes through the house. Mum is not impressed, although he did give her a kiss as the song goes: 'I saw mummy kissing Santa Claus underneath the mistletoe last night'. Mum was wearing glasses with mistletoe on saying kiss me', ha-ha.

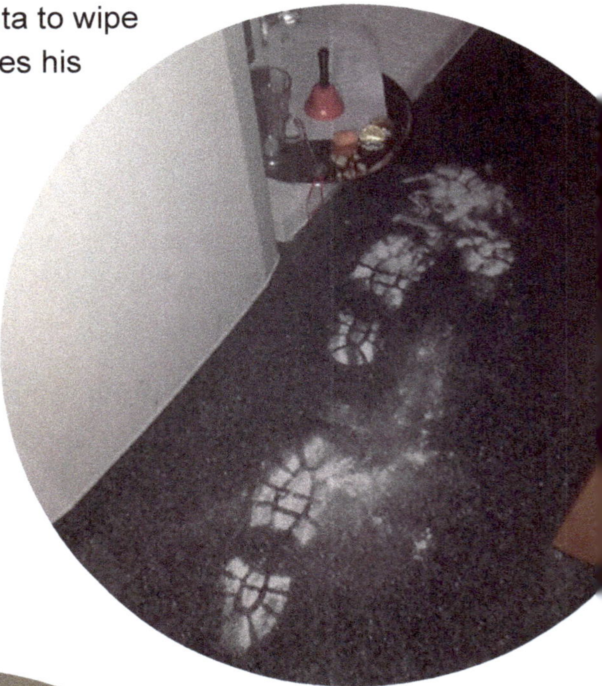

Dad was not happy, his bottom lip protruding like a little boy who'd lost his chocolate.

Faye Farmer

Before Mum and Dad went to sleep on the floor in the front room, where they stay every Christmas Eve to stop the kids coming down and opening the presents too early, she met with Lula Bell and Oscar the fairies as they had written letters for Niki and Jake. As they do on birthdays and Christmas, she put them in the stockings to add to the presents Santa had already put in there.

Goodnight Farmer family.

**Love you lots.**

*emo and derrick the elves*

# Day 25

**Christmas Day**

"IT'S CHRISTMAS, SANTA HAS BEEN, WAKE UP, WAKE UP", Mum shouts.

They all pile into mum and dads room to join Josh, you see Mum and Dad stay downstairs on Christmas Eve, as Josh stays in their room when he comes home for holidays, and to make sure the children don't sneak down in the middle of the night to look at the presents.

Although this year, the room seems so much smaller, as not only is the huge Josh home, we also have the very big Tom, Niki's boyfriend, over for Christmas from Holland. Santa even remembered he was with us, so his presents were delivered here too. See kids, Santa knows wherever you are.

Even Mum and Dad got stockings from Santa this time. I think he wanted to make it up to Dad for kissing Mum.

Stockings were opened and we all piled into the kitchen for bacon sandwiches for breakfast. Except Jake, he has difficulties trying new foods so stuck with toast. Now everyone was sent upstairs to put on their Christmas elf clothes. Mum was already dressed in her Mrs Clause dress that came from Santa as it didn't fit Mrs Clause this year because Santa took too many goodies from the children last Christmas Eve and fed them to her. Without this routine, no one was allowed in the front room to open their presents.

They were made to queue up, smallest to tallest, and Mum rang Santa's bell which means PRRRREEESSSEENNTTTS.

The sound of ripping paper flying through the air, the laughter and screams from the kids as they opened their presents, mum and dad trying to be fair making them take turns, things went pretty smoothly, although Jake wanted to take everything out of  there packaging and play with it. But Mum and Dad had to open their presents and the children always want to go off before they do, but Mum wanted them to learn patience. They all did so well this year, they even didn't meltdown and disappear before Mum and Dad finished.

Tom and Niki brought each other masks; one was a unicorn head and the other one a horse head. The enthusiasm with which they showed the actions and noises was comedy value.

Dinner was a hit, thank you to my hubby, Nik, it was delicious as usual. Emo and Derrick were so tired they took time to chill. They let Mummy Clause, Josh Elf and Tom Elf take over most of the elf duties. Tom Elf took care of Niki Elf; Josh Elf had Emo and Derrick sit with him but then, when he put them on the chair next to him, he accidentally buried them under wrapping paper and they nearly ended up in the bin. Good save, Jake spotted them and saved his elf friends. Between Tom Elf and Josh Elf the two tiny elves, Emo and Derrick, became squashed, and were not sure which of the bigger elves had made the smell, but they must have had Brussels in their stockings, he-he.

Derrick and Emo watched all the excitement and reported back to Santa what was happening after the Christmas dinner that was very filling, Dad, and really scrummy. They curled up under the Christmas tree and slept.

Good night, dear Farmer family.

**Love you all.**

emo and derrick the elves

# Day 26

Emo and Derrick took a morning selfie with Mum. She was so tired after staying up late with Dad and Emo and Derrick, while waiting for Santa the night before, you could see it in her face, the suitcases under her eyes, the hair a giant fluffy mess. Dad didn't mind the way she looked, as he was in the same position as Mum, but his bags were as big as skips.

Emo and Derrick were waiting by the phone for Grandad to phone as he and Hayley were coming round for dinner.

Emo and Derrick played Pokémon cards with Josh and Jake.

The Farmer family had a nice, relaxing day.

Later that evening, Emo and Derrick lay on the bed with Mum while waiting for Jake to join her.

They helped Mum to put curlers in her hair, then they wanted to try out Mum's new handbag Dad and the kids bought for her.

They used the handbag as a seat while Mum and Jake put on a movie, *Ice Age 5*: they loved the movie.

Even elf brothers argue over the remote sometimes. Mum was shaking her head at them.

Emo and Derrick were eating Jake's favourite biscuits while watching the movie.

Emo was still trying to be romantic and get Mum to go back to Lapland with him, but Mum just smiled and said no, as she is in love with Dad so he has no chance.

Emo and Derrick even asked if they could run her a bath with her bath bombs, but Mum said, "Thanks, I am a little busy right now." She was spending time with Jake looking through his microscope so she invited them to join in. Emo made his brother, Derrick, facepalm as he was making really rude noises with the whoopee cushion that Dad got in his stocking from Santa. They then hung out in Mum and Dad's stockings.

Emo was very
pleased his wish
come true and he
received some new shiny
white teeth; it made him never want to stop smiling.

Emo and Derrick said their prayers and put the window
decoration to show Santa they really had remembered
their prayers.

Good night sweet Farmer family.

**Love you all lots especially mum she is a star**

emo and derrick the elves xxx

# Day 27-28

Emo and Derrick were needed to help Santa clean up so there will be a double story tomorrow as today they have had too much to do. Mum thanked them for their help before they went.

# Day 29

Emo and Derrick helped Mum and Dad set up the house and garden ready for the guests, oh my goodness, the invasion of the Greeks. Mum, Emo and Derrick greeted everyone; Mum was dressed in her Mrs Clause outfit. The children's and the adults faces showed that Mum, Dad and the elves did a good job.

Lots of fun, games, food, music and dancing was had by all. Mum wants to say sorry for being a bit quiet and Emotional as she just wanted to please everyone and see everyone's smiles. The day was so special and it meant so much that their family had come because this has been such a hard year for them all. This was something that cheered up Mum, though, and took her tears away.

Mum thought she was more Emotional than the Emotional Elf. She took some time out so the children didn't see her cry. Her sister, Ellie, and niece, Mia, came to talk to her and they had the best news ever: Mia was going to have a new baby. It was enough to help Mum get her Emotions under control and go back to party with the elves

and her family. They played lots of games with no bad losers and they all rolled with laughter when Uncle Tony played pie face because he was being a child saying, "You can't get me," then wham, a face full of cream, lots of laughter from all happened as Niki followed, but all the rest of the children attacked him with handfuls of cream. Mum thinks it was the highlight of the day.

Mum and the elves sat with all the children to read Christmas stories before another huge amount of present opening began.

Mum loved playing pie face with the children and reading stories and hugging them tight, and they are all so polite. Dad did an amazing job on the food and entertaining everyone, Mum watched from afar as she still sometimes suffers with shyness, no matter how hard she tries not to be.

It was a perfect day. Mum wants to thank everyone for being themselves: beautiful, kind, loving, intelligent and amazing. The kids all wanted to stay, that is the best thing.

I want to say that Mum, Dad, Emo and Derrick had the best
visit: a new brother, Frederick, came to join them. We are
all so proud of Niki, Jake, Tom and Josh for helping to make
the day special, and by joining in even when it was busy and
loud, well done, you did Mum and Dad proud today.

Mum was telling the children all about the elf story she was
writing and that they are all in it, and little Rose seemed so
excited so I plan to put all the children in the book so that
it can be a Christmas story to
remember for the children
for years to come.
Oh, and Derrick
and Emo have a
new elf friend,
Frederick
the Elf.

He comes from the South Pole,
from a town called Yelwarc.

Good night
Farmer family.

Good night
Thomas, Rose,
Lilli, Ruby and
Patrick; Maria,
Patrick, Molly,
Izzie, Mia and
Matt; Ellie, Tony,
Anna, Cloe and
Sophia; Josh, Jake,
Niki, Tom, Mum and
Dad, Yia-Yia and Papou,
Bob, Laura and Olivia, who
we hope to meet again one day.
We are sad for those who were unable to attend, we love
you all. Emo, Derrick and Frederick the elves want to wish
you all the very best of nights. Thank you again for spending
time with the Farmer family.

emo, derrick and
fredrick the elves xxx

# Day 30

After a big day yesterday, Mum, Dad, Emo, Derrick and Frederick cleaned the kitchen. Josh and Jake cleaned the front room and Niki and Tom cleaned Niki's room. It's been a relaxing day, with Dad and Mum chilled, listening to music. Josh and Jake spent time together and, of course, Niki and Tom were spending time together. Niki and Tom sitting in a tree

K-i-s-s-i-n-g, he-he can't believe the cheeky elves sang that.

Emo, Derrick and Frederick
played spin the bottle with
the snowmen, notice
Emo had the kiss-me
glasses on. They
used a small, empty
medicine bottle, it
was empty because
they all had
headaches from the
day before and Mum
had to give them
the medicine to help.
(Don't try that at
home kids.)

Emo, Derrick and Frederick
decided it
was time to try and open
their own Facebook
account, so we're sitting
on the kitchen table with
Dad's laptop.

Next the elves hung out with Charlie's Angels.

After, Jake had a Pringle attack fight with Josh because Jake doesn't like to share his Pringles and Josh wanted one. Jake, Mum, Dad and Josh all settled down to watch *Ice Age 5,* what a lovely day was had by all.

Good night, dear Farmer family.

Love you lots. The fun begins tomorrow, New Year's Eve. Let's kick 2016 into oblivion and make this year really count.

*emo, derrick and fredrick the elves xxx*

# Day 31

Emo, Derrick and Frederick are so glad dad, Josh and grandad saw the New Year in together; male bonding. Mum looked after Hayley, Jake Skyped his friends and Niki and Tom spent time together.

Emo, Derrick and Fredrick took a selfie, and Mum then joined the angels for the Greek dance. Next, they did their own Village People dance, and they did the window display before finally counting the New Year in with Mum, Niki, Tom, Hayley and Jake, as the clock struck midnight. For the first time ever, Niki got to spend it kissing her boyfriend, as he lives in Holland and she wanted their first New Year's Eve to be as romantic as the movies. A moment I think she and Tom will carry with them forever.

Good night sweet Farmer family and extended family, I love you all.

It turns out Emo, Derrick and Fredrick will not be going back to the North or South Poles, the Farmer family would miss them too much. There won't be daily posts, but the kids want them to stick around to also share our special occasions with and to spend more family time with all our extended family, two new members and older members, because Mum really likes them.

**HAPPY NEW YEAR.**

**Love you all.**

*emo, derrick and frederick the elves here we are!*

# January 1st
## 2017

It is Emo, Derrick and Frederick, the elves' last day
of storytelling.

There will be trips with the kids throughout the next year
as they have been officially adopted by the Farmer family;
no one wants them to leave because they have become
so important. They have found a new mum they even did a
window display to show it.

Emo, Derrick and Fredrick joined Mum and Dad for coffee this morning before Mum and the elves went to visit Yia-Yia for coffee and to pick up some presents before Josh and Tom have to return to their homes.

While they were there, they noticed Yia-Yia needed some help with wrapping presents for her visitors that day, so they made quick work with wrapping and placing presents under the tree for Yia-Yia's guests.

Mum had a lovely ham sandwich and coffee before returning home with her elf friends.

When they got home, they helped Josh and Mum gets his clothes all washed and cleaned ready to take back home with him.

They hung out with Jake's Pokémon before taking a ride on a giant catapult that Dad got Jake for Christmas. Emo, Derrick and Fredrick watched *The BFG* movie with Mum, Dad and Jake.

Emo, Derrick and Frederick decided to use the warm socks Yia-Yia bought them for Christmas as sleeping bags before making new window displays.

So, goodbye, sweet Farmer family, it has been a wonderful journey we have been on and a great Christmas.

Adding family to this, my book,
and sharing our story,
to bring closeness to
our family and the
extended family, and
to help them also
understand why we
stopped going out or
to their houses, was
not because we didn't
want to go, but because
of the anxiety our children
were having and how difficult
it was for us as a family coming to
terms with the diagnosis, ourselves as parents, and for the
children themselves, has been a really important part.

So goodbye for now, Farmer family.

**We love you all so much.**

emo the emotional elf and
his brothers derrick and fredrick
xxxx

**THE END**

A book filled with love, laughter and so much fun.
What is this book supposed to do, raise awareness
and say goodbye?

The book is about issues, a book about good times and hard times, to help bring things up with children to minimise the shock of loss. The ability to accept change is OK. We wanted to teach them to be kind, loving and compassionate. To help them regain a sense of control, to help ease their anxiety, to build their self-esteem and to encourage wellbeing.

I want to give each of them a sense of self-worth and self-respect.

Our family is made up of two cultures, English and Greek. The Greek side of the family are all equally as important as the English Hord side, my family are all different. Different backgrounds and different upbringings, but all equal in my love for them and each and every one of them bring a special quality to me, Nik and the kids.

Sometimes they can annoy me and make me want to pull my hair out, but that's family, I wouldn't want it any other way or any different. I love you all just as you are.

I would also like to add that Olivia, our beautiful niece, we haven't been able to get to know you sweetheart, and haven't seen you since you were eight. That was not your fault.

But circumstances that mean sometimes people go their separate ways for a good reason and sometime kids miss out. I am sorry that happened to you, but you do have a family that loves you more than you will ever know and a lot of hearts hurt without you in their lives. The last picture I have is with you and my children at Yia-Yia's house, you had the biggest most beautiful smile, you were a princess, the apple of your dad's eye. Maybe one day you will be able to understand that adults sometimes mess up, they make mistakes, feelings get hurt and hearts break. That can make you not able to put things right, even for the kids.

Interpretations sometimes get muddled and hurt feelings get bypassed until you forget the good things, and there were many when you were little. Your dad loved you so much, just as much as your sisters.

He just had a hurt heart without you.

Our story and journey will continue with ups and downs that will never change, as that is real life.

Slightly more difficult for our family given all we go through, but we will grow stronger and fight with everything we have, for change for us and for a change to how we are treated.

This story has been so hard to write and put together as I have struggled with punctuation and writing my whole life, but I don't want my children to see their mum doesn't try, because how can I expect them to give their all if I don't? How can I expect them to be confident if I'm not?

It is the end chapter to a very difficult time for me and my husband and children. We have been on a journey of autism diagnosis with our children. This book is written to tell my family, that despite our challenges and unique personalities, we are perfect the way we are, we don't need to change that for anyone, or wait on others for approval.

We are us, and that's OK.

We will share our life with anyone who is willing to understand that.

We will make new friendships and we will achieve what is destined for us to achieve even if our days are up and down, whether we talk or not. We have each other, in failures and success; we will pick each other up and give space when needed.

I adore each and every one of you and I always will

I am mum, wife, daughter, sister, aunt, granddaughter cousin and niece. I am a carer, but most importantly, I am me a unique and special, loving girl with a heart of gold who is always there.

I AM MRS FAYE KERRY FARMER

I AM AND WILL ALWAYS BE PROUD OF THAT FACT

There is someone special to me who is not in any photo in this book as she passed, and the only photo we have is our own and we can't share that. Amy Farmer, daughter of Nik Farmer and Faye Farmer, sister to Joshua, Niki and Jacob, but I want a part of her in this, too, as this is for them all, so here is the only part I can share.

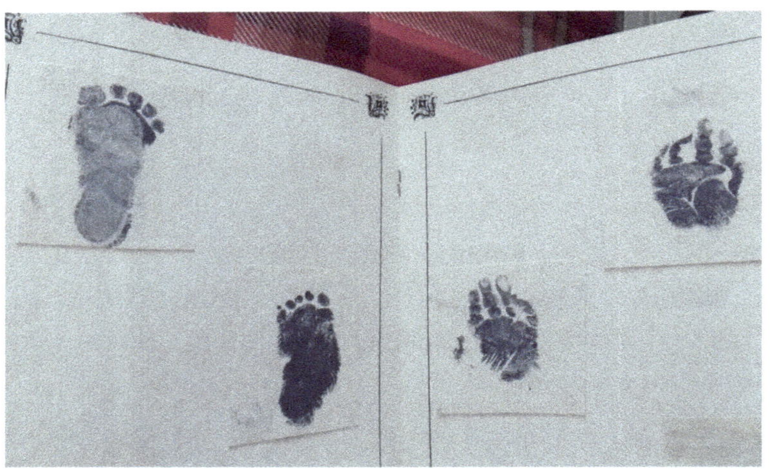

Goodbye, our baby girl is at peace. Amy was born 24 June 1996 and lived for 25 minutes. Mummy, Daddy, Joshua, Niki and Jake all love, miss and think of you always.

There are also others I want to honour in my book, and because I would like to highlight those that have shaped my life and helped make me who I am – so here goes.

John and Frances Stark, my beautiful grandparents, who shaped my life and accepted me for who I am, and were proud of me. They taught me so much.

Violette Hord, my father's mum, and Henry Hord, my father's dad.

I never got to meet my grandfather, Henry, but what I do know is he was a hard-working man who liked children enough to have eleven of them.

Violette, my grandmother, was the first one we knew of to be diagnosed with Huntington's disease, which set our family down a path of great torment and loss. So, in honour of those that have died and those still affected and those that will be affected, I will mention them so their lives were not in vain and not forgotten.

The next to pass away was James Hord, also known and loved as Jimmy, David Hord the blue-eyed handsome charmer and an amazing chef.

Christine Sonko, who recently passed and it's still so raw. Her death was unnecessary at that point in her life. It has left everyone with more questions and so much anger, hurt and additional pain. We knew she would get worse and pass, just not like this. She was a lover of life, married a lot and produced beautiful children who stayed by her side all the way to the end – we will have the answers and justice. Christine was the rose of the family and my childhood best friend. Just before the visit to the publishers, Susan Hord sadly passed away, too, leaving her children and grandchildren with a few unanswered questions. The healing for them will be harder, but know your mum loved you all.

Those still suffering, Pauline Hord, June Hord and Mark Hord. Those who don't have the illness, but still suffer the effects of seeing their loved ones slowly get worse, Vi Hord, a smart, quiet woman; Michael Hord,  the betting man who recently passed suddenly and is now with his step-son, Darren, known for the children's sake as the 'double rainbows'.

Barbara Hord, the hard-working woman, wife, mum and grandmother.

Then there is John Hord, my daddy, the pillar of the family, the one classed as the head of the family, the strong one, the 'go to' man, the fisherman, the grandad my kids and I adore.

But also the man who frustrates me over his parking spaces. He is married to Odette Hord, my mother, they are no longer a couple, but she runs the family from afar.

She was the carer of the family and sorts all of us out, including my dad, even now. Also, a big thank you to Marty Griffith for watching over my mum and taking great care of her when we can't be there. There are too many kids between them all, and their kids, to name.

So, for all of you, it has taken so much. Live your life, don't worry about 'what ifs' just keep being strong and carry on. You have the power within you to go on and have the most fantastic life, even if faced with issues beyond your control, don't let this illness define you.

There was my great-uncle, Albi, who could drink anyone under the table. He loved to sing and was good. I loved him so much. Then there was Aunty Magaret who loved bossing us about, her son, David, who had a troubled life, but still he mattered. Then there was Albi's brother, David. He was a hard-working man who survived cancer only to go downhill and find out very late he had Huntington's.

So, that is one of the causes close to my heart.

The others are autism, Tourette's, mental health issues; be it anxiety, depression or others, they all need highlighting. There is also epilepsy, cerebral palsy, Prader Willi syndrome and Down's syndrome.

Heart issues, diabetes, strokes and hypermobility – the list is long and really I want to highlight many more, but these are the main ones that affect my family personally.

This is how I see it; society demands we keep things secret and not talk about certain issues because society as a whole is uncomfortable with it.

It doesn't matter whether there is a disability or ability, it's not the person that has to change, it's society and how we are so unaccepting of things people have no control over. If they could click their fingers and make it disappear, even those suffering, then they would.

We are in a time where many of these things are being highlighted, maybe because many have suffered in silence, too ashamed or embarrassed to ask for help. The only way we have a chance in life is to take our little voices and our slow burning candles and shine so brightly for a new inclusive life, for all, and acceptance for all; that is the only way the world will heal and become one community, one soul and one race, human.

I don't want to cure my kids of their difficulties, I want to show them that no matter what life sends their way they can still go on being just them.

I would also like to say a special thanks to my husband, Nikolas David Farmer, my love, my soul, my hero, he's funny and annoying and strong and gentle. He is kind, passionate, an amazingly intelligent man.

He is little weird, but my kind of weird, he can command a room just with his voice when he walks in, you look up and take notice. His belief in me and my ability, the way he has put up with all the challenges life has thrown our way. He lost his wife, she slowly got overtaken, the difficulties of grief and life nearly made her really ill and he gave her the biggest kick she needed to find herself again, and I am so glad he did or I would never have had the courage to change the things I needed to change, to lift myself back up and start shining again. The best thing he told me is that this book is my glory, uniquely mine, no one can take it from me – it is me.

His family have been a huge part of my life, and equally important to me as they are Greek and strong willed and stubborn, beautiful, unique people, they sometimes really frustrate me. But I still wouldn't change any of them ever. I would also like to mention my Greek nieces and nephews: Mia, Matt, Maria and Patrick, Bob and Laura and the very gorgeous Isabella, Anna and Olivia.

Great-nieces and nephews, Thomas, Patrick, Noah, Rose, Lily, Molly, Chloe and Sophia, I love you a lot. Tony and Ellie, I am so proud to be your sister-in-law. My other parents, my in-laws, my children's grandparents, Nikoleta and Theo, thank you for all your help over the years.

A big hello to my English family!! First my brothers, John and Chris, then there is their wives, Sam and Helen. Next there is my sister, Hayley, who I work as a carer, with nieces, Becky, Ellie, Holly, nephew little Tommy, Molly, Emma and Charlotte, and my little cousins who donated their time to help raise the funds for publishing this book; Grace and Mille, as promised you are in my book.

I would also like to say a very big thank you to my connections on many social media, neighbours and family and our friends that have donated and helped me to raise money for this book. Thanks so very much from the bottom of my heart.

Then there are my children: Amy, who was mentioned at the beginning of the dedications; Joshua Nikolas Farmer, his knowledge started with his dad when he made a board of knowledge with maths problems and challenges written on it every night, from a very young age. As my other kids say, he's a walking google, he is so smart, funny and intelligent, a born leader. He has a zest for life, an adult before his time. He is our first-born, the first couple of weeks were so hard as he had to have an op, but as soon as he did, he didn't stop growing. He loves super heroes, especially Superman.

He has an ability to teach himself what he wants to learn.

His dad and I were so proud standing watching him graduate with a first in business from Warwick University.

We were even prouder when he got a job straight after; this boy will go far.

Next, what can I say about Nikoletta Sophia Farmer? What a girl, she has had this very special personality since she was in my tummy.

She came slightly early after a bumpy pregnancy, and then having apnoea when she was born was very scary indeed. She kept the nurses busy, as soon as they walked away she would kick her tiny little foot and set off the alarms, when the nurses went over she would smile. This happened from almost day one with her. She is so beautiful and funny and smart, extremely one of a kind.

She is really happy that she has a boyfriend, Tom, now, and the change in her since has been great, she is blossoming into a beautiful woman, capable of doing anything she wants and probably more than she realises.

Yet I cannot even say just how much she means to our lives and how much I love her just as she is.

Jacob Theo Farmer, what can I say about Jacob? He is my youngest and was the most intuitive and sensitive boy from the moment he was born.

You could see his smart mind and kind personality, my little flappy bird, he doesn't sit still. He was counting from very young and, like his mum, liked escaping out of his room and you knew when he was awake as you would hear the stair gate being lifted. Always counting, and his knowledge of dinosaurs when he was little was immense. The little boy

who loved to read encyclopaedias and one time brought the entire dictionary home from class so no one was smarter than him. He loves talking to adults and sometimes finds it easier than with people his own age. But he is now working hard to change that. The one thing I really love is that he has this very competitive streak when he gets with his grandad, especially with fishing, and so far has been beating his grandad every time. He loves to rub grandad's nose in it. Jake is now doing kung fu and is in the black belt training class. He will be a black belt before we know it and it has been important for his confidence.

Jake and Niki were diagnosed with autism and anxiety, Jake has vasovagal syncope, this is the most challenging of his issues, and Niki has a Tourette's diagnosis as well.

Thank you for reading and I really hope you enjoyed getting to know our family.

mrs faye kerry farmer